BRANCH LINES TO DUNSTABLE

Sue and Geoff Woodward

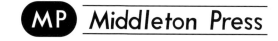
MP Middleton Press

Front Cover: On 24th April 1965, the final day of service on the Hatfield to Dunstable Branch, locomotive D8046 and two quad-art sets awaited permission to depart from Dunstable North station with "The Last Skimpot Flyer". As a farewell gesture, the headboard and a wreath were donated by the South Beds Locomotive Club. (G.I.Denn)

Back Cover: This panoramic view of Dunstable North station, with its busy goods yard, was taken in 1957 from the steps of the old LNWR signal box. Opened in 1866, the station was the meeting point of trains from both the Leighton Buzzard and Hatfield branch lines. These lines stopped carrying passengers within a few years of each other in the 1960s, although freight traffic continued for several years on different sections of the branches. Eventually parts of both became footpaths and cycleways. (B.Parnall)

Published May 2008

ISBN 978 1 906008 27 7

© *Middleton Press, 2008*

Design Deborah Esher

Published by
    Middleton Press
    Easebourne Lane
    Midhurst
    West Sussex
    GU29 9AZ
Tel: 01730 813169
Fax: 01730 812601
Email: info@middletonpress.co.uk
www.middletonpress.co.uk

Printed & bound by Biddles Ltd, Kings Lynn

INDEX

ACKNOWLEDGEMENTS

We are grateful to G.Croughton for supplying tickets and to A.R.Carder, N.Langridge and Mr D and Dr S Salter for proof reading.

I. Route diagram.

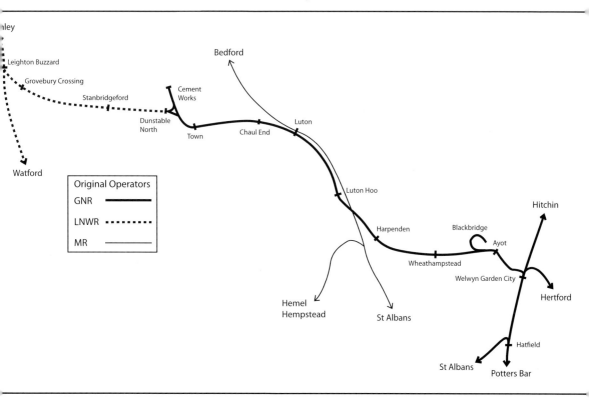

GEOGRAPHICAL SETTING

Our journey starts at Leighton Buzzard on the Upper Greensand, which was of great commercial importance in the district. This strata underlies the Chalk of the Chiltern Hills onto which the line climbs at 1 in 40 on its approach to Dunstable. It descends to Luton and continues mainly on Chalk to Hatfield.

From Luton to Wheathampstead, the route is in close company with the east flowing River Lea and it crosses it on the approach to Hatfield. Between these places, it passes close to Welwyn Garden City, which was developed from 1920 onwards. There was woodland in this area, but most of the line was surrounded by agricultural land, which generated much railway traffic.

The western part of the journey was in Bedfordshire, trains passing into Hertfordshire 1½ miles north of Harpenden.

The maps are to the scale of 25ins to 1 mile, with north at the top, unless otherwise indicated.

HISTORICAL BACKGROUND

Before the arrival of a railway in the Hertfordshire and Bedfordshire area manufacturers, coal merchants, farmers and the owners of country estates had to transport their raw materials and other necessities overland by horse and cart from the canal at Hemel Hempstead or Leighton, which involved many man hours and only relatively small loads could be carried. Therefore, as soon as the London to Birmingham railway became a reality in 1838, thoughts turned to connecting the towns of Luton and Dunstable with it.

George and Robert Stephenson devised a plan to do just that, but at a meeting in 1844 it was rejected by the people of Luton, on the grounds of too much disruption to certain parts of the town. However, the residents of Dunstable were receptive to the idea and forged ahead with the Stephensons' proposals to create a branch line from Leighton to their town, obtaining an Act of Parliament in 1845. By that time the London & North Western Railway Company had become the proprietors of the London & Birmingham line and were in favour of a branch line to Dunstable. Having altered the plans to give less steep gradients, it was built and opened for freight on 29th May 1848 and passengers on 1st June, operated by the LNWR.

Luton industrialists desired a direct line to London, but found themselves in the largest town in the country without a rail or water connection, isolated between the LNWR to the west and the Great Northern Railway being built a few miles to the east. It is not difficult to understand their willingness to compromise by connecting with that new railway (being a more direct route than via the LNW) and a plan was prepared for a branch line with a junction at Welwyn. The shareholders of the Hertford & Welwyn Junction Railway Company were informed of the plan, with the suggestion that it could achieve an extension of their line, to create a link between the LNWR, the GNR and the Eastern Counties Railway Company at Hertford. The GNR decided to step in and offered to work such a line, but would not back it financially.

Accordingly, an Act of Parliament was obtained on 16th July 1855 giving authority for the Luton, Dunstable & Welwyn Junction Railway, allowing connections with the LNWR at Dunstable, the GNR at Digswell (Welwyn) and a bridge to carry the new line over the main line to join the Hertford branch. However, it was the section between Luton and Dunstable which took priority and, despite initial dificulties with the LNWR, it opened for freight on 5th April 1858 and passengers on 3rd May, basically as an extension of the Leighton to Dunstable branch.

On 28th June 1858 the Luton, Dunstable & Welwyn Junction Railway Company amalgamated with the Hertford & Welwyn Junction Railway Company to become the Hertford, Luton & Dunstable Railway Company, by which time the former had issued notices to purchase land for their line, but could not finance it. A request to the LNWR to lease the line was rejected and, in any case, plans to join the Hertford branch with the Dunstable branch came to nothing when the GNR imposed conditions which made it impossible to put a bridge over their main line.

Although construction had commenced at the Welwyn end in 1856, there was little progress by 1858. However, after a second 'turning of the sod' ceremony in January 1859, the company received a Parliamentary extension of time in July which allowed them to successfully complete the work. The new section between Welwyn Junction and Luton opened for passengers and freight on 1st September 1860, with trains for Hatfield using the main line (until December 1868 when a separate track for the branch was opened alongside).

With everything in place the GNR decided, for strategic reasons, to take over the Dunstable branch and it was absorbed into their network by an Act passed on 12th June 1861, although a clause allowed the LNWR to continue sending traffic between Dunstable and Luton.

Although the GNR and the LNWR worked reasonably well together, they found difficulty in agreeing station arrangements at Dunstable. In the end the LNWR agreed to replace their existing station, and built the one which later became Dunstable North, opening in 1866. For their part, the GNR rebuilt the small station at Dunstable Church Street, but that burnt down in September 1871 and was replaced by a much larger building. In the early 1860s Luton station had been enlarged with an extra island platform and the temporary stations at Harpenden and Wheathampstead were replaced by permanent buildings. By 1895 the GNR needed to widen its main lines between Hatfield and Digswell, which necessitated using the old branch line as the new down slow line, and a new track was laid for the branch.

Between 1880 and 1890 up to 500 season ticket holders travelled on the Hatfield branch and, although people campaigned for the line to be doubled, only a section through Luton was constructed and opened in September 1899. In 1914 the Hatfield branch was described as 'such a profitable line', due in all probability to the number of businesses with private sidings, who received and dispatched very varied and extensive traffic. Particularly important were the chalk quarries near Dunstable, the sand and gravel pits in the Leighton area and Vauxhall Motors in Luton.

The railway companies were grouped into the so-called 'Big Four' in 1923, at which time the Leighton to Dunstable branch came under the control of the London Midland & Scottish Railway Company and the Hatfield to Dunstable line was the responsibility of the London & North Eastern Railway. Following railway nationalisation in 1948, British Railways Eastern Region were responsible for the Hatfield branch as far as Harpenden down distant signal, and from there to Leighton came under the London Midland Region.

Many different types of steam locomotives and rolling stock found their way on to the branches over the years, but by February 1958 three diesel shunters had been commissioned for use at Luton and the first diesel hauled freight train ran in February 1959, followed by a Birmingham Sulzer in June. English Electrics took over most of the passenger working on the Hatfield branch from 6th June 1960, but were superseded by diesel multiple units after one was successfully tested there in 1962.

On the Leighton branch in the 1950s, passenger numbers declined and BR took the decision to terminate passenger services from 2nd July 1962. Freight traffic continued to run to Dunstable until 1st January 1966, but even then a short length from Grovebury to Leighton was kept open for the sand traffic. Track was lifted from Dunstable in 1968 and took until 1969 to clear as far as Stanbridgeford. BR closed the line completely on 5th December 1969 and by 1971 all the track had been lifted. Since then parts of the route have been taken over as a footpath and cycleway, and some station areas have disappeared under new buildings.

The Hatfield line was scheduled to lose its passenger service on 6th January 1965 but, because of local pressure, was reprieved - but only until 24th April. From then on, freight trains still ran into Blackbridge sidings and the line between Luton and Dunstable was kept open for cement traffic, after a connection was put in from the Midland main line.

Track was removed from the redundant length between Luton East and Blackbridge in 1966. Bridges were dismantled and associated buildings were demolished or burned. The closure of Blackbridge sidings in May 1971 allowed railway land to be incorporated into the new A1(M). Eventually most of the Hatfield to Luton section was adopted as a country path.

PASSENGER SERVICES

Leighton Buzzard - Dunstable

The service appears to have been mostly weekdays only, with four return trips in the early years. From 1860, seven trains a day was the norm until the 1930s, when one of them became Saturdays only.

In the final years there were only three trains each day, with one extra on Saturdays.

Dunstable - Hatfield

Weekday frequencies are discussed herein. Initially there were five trains when the line only ran to Luton. Upon completion there were six, this figure increasing to ten by 1910. The figure was down to eight in 1936 and seven in 1950. There were two or three Sunday trains in most years, but these terminated at Dunstable Town.

Most trains from Leighton Buzzard ran through to Luton while most from Hatfield continued to Dunstable. Thus in the heyday of the branches, there were 17 or 18 trains between Dunstable and Luton.

We include a sample of Hobbs timetable, which is one of few to show the composite service and is particularly worthy of study. There were through trains to and from Kings Cross until the end, but the use of bold type in this extract is inconsistent.

Goods Man., John Ashley.] HERTFORD, HATFIELD, LUTON, and DUNSTABLE.—G. N. [Asst. Goods Man., R. H. Twelvetrees.

June 1869

February 1890

July 1910

HERTFORD, HATFIELD, LUTON, and DUNSTABLE.—Great Northern.

LEIGHTON, DUNSTABLE, and LUTON.—London and North Western.

HATFIELD, LUTON, and DUNSTABLE.—Great Northern.

Miles	Down.	Week Days.																			Sundays.			
		mrn	mrn	mrn	mrn	mrn	mrn	aft	mrn	aft	aft	aft	aft	aft	aft	aft	aft	aft	aft	aft	mrn	mrn	aft	aft
	354London (King's Cross) dep.	....	....	....	7 45	9 20	....	....	1145	Saturdays only.	1 15	2 30	4 20	5 10	5 49	....	7 0	....	....	10 0	....	8 50	....	7 0
—	Hatfield ... dep.	....	....	....	8 25	9 51	....	....	1225		2 0	3 18	4 54	5 40	6 28	....	7 33	....	....	1042	....	9 33	....	7 37
4½	Ayot	....	....	....	8 35	10 0	....	....	1235		2 10	3 27	5 4	5 53	6 38	....	7 43	....	....	1052	....	9 43	....	7 47
7½	Wheathampstead	....	....	....	8 41	10 6	....	....	1241		2 16	3 33	5 10	5 59	6 44	....	7 49	....	....	1058	....	9 49	....	7 54
9½	Harpenden	....	....	....	8 50	1011	....	....	1246		2 21	3 38	5 15	6 4	6 49	....	7 54	....	....	11 3	....	9 54	....	7 59
12	Luton Hoo ‖	....	....	....	8 55	1016	....	....	1251		2 26	3 43	5 20	6 9	6 54	....	7 59	....	....	11 8	....	10 0	....	8 4
15	Luton 538, 549 arr.	....	....	....	9 3	1023	....	....	1258		2 34	3 50	5 27	6 16	7 1	....	8 6	....	....	1115	....	10 7	....	8 12
	Luton 538, 549 dep.	6 25	7 31	8 40	9 6	1026	11 7	1220	1 5	1 30	2 40	3 53	5 30	6 23	7 3	7 55	8 10	9 15	1015	1120	7 29	1012	5 22	8 22
19½	Dunstable (Church St.)	6 35	7 42	8 50	9 15	1037	1117	1230	1 15	1 40	2 51	4 4	5 41	6 34	7 16	8 6	8 21	9 26	1027	1131	7 40	1021	5 32	8 31
20½	" (L. & N. W.) .. arr.	6 39	7 46	8 55	9 20	1040	1121	1235	1 18	1 45	2 54	4 7	5 44	6 37	7 21	8 11	8 24	9 29	1031	1134	....	....	....	....
27½	435 Leighton ... arr.	7 30	....	9 15	....	....	1140	1 22	....	....	3 17	....	6 25	....	....	8 30	....	....	....	....	....	....	....	....

‖ Station at New Mill End, 1½ miles from Luton Hoo.

July 1910

LEIGHTON BUZZARD, DUNSTABLE, and LUTON.

Miles.		Week Days only.						
		mrn	mrn	mrn	aft	aft	aft	aft
	452 London (Euston) ... dep.	5 25	8 35	10 50	12A15	2 5	6B37	7 15
—	Leighton Buzzard ... dep.	7 45	1020	12 28	2 15	4 50	7 15	9 22
4½	Stanbridgeford	7 53	1030	12 37	2 24	4 59	7 23	9 32
7	Dunstable (L.M.S.) arr.	8 0	1039	12 45	2 32	5 7	7 31	9 41
	Dunstable (L.M.S.) dep.	8 2	1048	12 48	3 47	5 17	7 33	1017
8	Dunstable Town	8 6	1052	12 52	3 52	5 21	7 37	1021
12½	Luton (L.N.E.) 865 ... arr.	8 15	11 1	1 1	4 1	5 30	7 46	1030

Miles		Week Days only.								
		mrn	mrn	mrn	aft	aft	aft	aft		aft
	Luton (L.N.E.) ... dep.	6 20	8 30	1120	1220	2 42	5 39	8 0	Saturdays only.	9 53
4½	Dunstable Town	6 31	8 40	1131	1231	2 53	5 50	8 11		10 4
5½	Dunstable (L.M.S.) arr.	6 34	8 45	1134	1234	2 56	5 53	8 14		10 7
	Dunstable (L.M.S.) dep.	6 50	8 48	1138	1 5	3 10	6 0	8 18		1012
8¼	Stanbridgeford 458	6 59	8 57	1147	1 14	3 19	6 12	8 27		1021
12½	Leighton Buzzard 412, arr.	7 10	9 6	1156	1 23	3 28	6 23	8 36		1030
52¾	458 London (Euston) ... arr.	8 37	10 15	1 45	4F27	5 35	8 5	10 50		1152

NOTES.

A Departs at 12 50 aft. on Sats.
B Departs at 5 32 aft. on Saturdays.
F Arrives at 2 26 aft. on Thursdays & 2 50 aft. on Saturdays.

November 1930

H. Preston, Station Master, Luton.]

WEEK DAYS.

DOWN.	a.m	a.m	a.m	a.m	a.m	a.m	p.m	a.m	p.m	p.m	p.m	p.m	p.m	p.m	p.m	p.m	p.m	p.m	p.m
KING'S CROSS dep.	...	...	...	7 45	9 17	...	...	1130	...	1 A 3	...	4 15	5 10	5T54	...	6 55	...	9s10	...
Finsbury Park „	......	......	......	7 53	9 23	......	......	1137	......	1 A 9	......	4 23	......	6 T 1	......	7 2	......	9s17	......
Hatfield ... „	...	...	...	8 25	9 51	...	...	1215	...	2 0	...	4 57	5 38	6 40	...	7 46	...	9s53	...
Welwyn G.C. „	......	......	......	8 31	9 57	......	......	1221	......	2 6	......	5 3	5 46	6 46	......	7 52	......	9s59	......
Ayot ... ... „	...	...	...	8 37	10 3	...	...	1227	...	2 12	...	5 9	5H56	6 52	...	7 58	...	10 s 4	...
Wheath'mpst' „	......	......	......	8 43	10 9	......	......	1233	......	2 18	......	5 15	6 2	6 58	......	8 4	......	10s10	......
Harpenden „	...	...	...	8 49	1014	...	...	1238	...	2 23	...	5 20	6 8	7 4	...	8 9	...	10s15	...
Luton Hoo ... „	......	......	......	8 54	1019	......	......	1243	......	2 28	......	5 25	6 15	7 9	......	8 14	......	10s20	......
LUTON, L.N.E. a.	...	...	...	9 2	1026	...	...	1250	...	2 36	...	5 32	6 22	7 16	...	8 21	...	10s27	...
LUTON, L.N.E. d.	6 20	7 34	8 30	9 6	1029	1120	1220	1 0	1s30	2 42	4 0	5 39	6 30	7 20	8 0	8 23	9 53	STOP	11 0
Dunstable Town	6 31	7 45	8 40	9 17	1040	1131	1231	1 11	1s41	2 53	4 11	5 50	6 41	7 31	8 11	8 34	10 4		11P13
„ L.M.S. a.	6 34	7 48	8 43	9 20	1043	1134	1234	1 14	1s44	2 56	4 14	5 53	6 44	7 34	8 14	8 37	10 7	p.m	11s13
„ „ d.	6 50	—	8 45	—	—	1138	1 5	—	—	3 5	—	6 0	—	—	8 18	—	☞	10s12	—
Stanbridgeford „	6 59	......	8 54	......	......	1147	1 14	......	......	3 14	......	6 14	......	......	8 27	......	......	10s21	......
Leighton Buz. a.	7 10	...	9 3	...	...	1156	1 23	...	...	3 23	...	6 23	...	...	8 36	...	...	10C30	...

UP.	a.m	a.m	a.m	a.m	a.m	a.m	a.m	p.m	p.m	p.m	p.m	p.m	p.m	p.m	p.m	p.m	p.m	p.m
Leighton Buzzard d.	...	...	7 35	...	...	1020	...	1228	...	2 15	...	4 50	...	7 18	...	...	9s48	...
Stanbridgeford „	......	......	7 43	......	......	1030	......	1237	......	2 24	......	4 59	......	7 28	......	......	9s59	......
Dunstable, arr.	...	...	7 50	...	...	1039	...	1245	...	2 32	...	5 7	...	7 36	...	...	10 s 7	...
„ L.M.S. dep.	6 0	7 11	7 55	8 15	9 30	1048	11 5	1248	1 50	☞	3 47	5 17	6 15	7 40	7 49	8 55	10 17	11s20
„ Town „	6 5	7 15	7 59	8 19	9 34	1052	11 9	1252	1 54	...	3 52	5 21	6 19	7 44	7 53	8 59	10 21	11s24
LUTON, L.N.E. arr.	6 15	7 24	8 8	8 28	9 43	11 1	11 18	1 1	2 [illegible]	......	4 1	5 30	6 28	7 53	8 2	9 8	10 30	11s33
LUTON, L.N.E. dep.	—	7 26	—	8 35	—	—	11 20	1 6	—	...	4 3	5 34	6 47	—	8 25	—	10s55	—
Luton Hoo ... „	......	7 32	......	8 42	......	......	11 26	1 12	......	......	4 9	5 40	6 54	......	8 31	......	11 s 2	......
Harpenden ... „	...	7 37	...	8 48	...	...	11 31	1 17	...	...	4 15	5 45	7 3	...	8 36	...	11 s 8	...
Wheathampstead „	......	7 42	......	8 53	......	......	11 36	1 22	......	......	4 20	5 49	7 8	......	8 41	......	11s13	......
Ayot ... ... „	...	7 48	...	8 59	...	...	11 42	1 28	...	...	4 26	5 55	7 14	...	8 47	...	11s20	...
Welwyn G. City „	......	7 52	......	9 3	......	......	11 46	1 32	......	......	4 30	5F59	7 20	......	8 51	......	11s24	......
Hatfield ... arr.	...	7 58	...	9 10	...	...	11 52	1 38	...	...	4 38	6 5	7 29	...	8 57	...	11s30	...
Finsbury Park „	......	8 29	......	9 37	......	......	12 38	2D23	......	......	5 32	6B39	7 59	......	9 52	......	—	......
KING'S CROSS ... „	...	8 35	...	9 44	...	...	12 45	2D31	...	...	5 44	6F37	8 6	...	9 59	...	...	...

NOTES.

A Sats. 4 mins. later.
B Sats. arr. 7.1.
C Arr. Bletchley 11.21 (Sats. 11.24).
D Sats. 12 mins. earlier.
F Change at Welwyn G.C. to arrive King's Cross 6.37.
H Arr. 5.50 p.m.
P Sats. 11.10.
s Sats. only.
T Or 8 mins. later, Sats. excepted, change at Welwyn G.C.
Heavy type—through trains.

Hobbs timetable for January 1936

HATFIELD, LUTON, and DUNSTABLE

Third class only, except where otherwise shown

Miles		Week Days																	Sundays			
		a.m	a.m	a.m	p.m E	a.m S	p.m S	p.m E	p.m S	p.m	p.m S	p.m E	p.m E	p.m S	p.m E	p.m S	p.m K	p.m F	a.m		p.m	p.m
	8a London (King's C.) dep	6 30	..	7 18	..	11A10	12B15	1 0	1 12	..	4A10	4B23	5B10	5X15	5B39	6B24	6F40	6F49	8A20	..	12A5	7A10
—	Hatfield ... dep	7 25	..	8 20	..	12 8	12 48	2 10	2 15	..	5 0	5U0	5B42	6 7	6 7	6B55	7F12	7F22	9 30	..	1 10	7 45
2½	Welwyn Garden City	7 31	..	8§31	..	12 14	12 55	2 17	2 25	..	5 7	5‖15	5 51	6T15	6T15	7V14	7 20	7 30	9 37	..	1 17	7 52
7½	Wheathampstead	7 48	..	8 48	..	12 26	1 9	2 29	2 37	..	5 19	5 27	6 3	6 32	6 32	7 28	7 33	7 43	9 50	..	1 30	8 5
9½	Harpenden	7 54	..	8 54	..	12 31	1 15	2 35	2 43	..	5 25	5 33	6K16	6 38	6 38	7 34	7K45	7K55	9 56	..	1 36	8 11
12	Luton Hoo H	8 0	..	9 0	..	..	1 21	2 41	2 49	..	5 31	5 39	6 22	..	6 44	7 40	7 51	8 1	10 2	..	1 42	8 17
15	Luton arr	8 6	..	9 6	..	12 41	1 28	2 47	2 55	..	5 38	5 46	6 28	6 48	6 50	7 46	7 57	8 7	10 9	..	1 49	8 24
	Luton dep	..	8 30	9 12	1250	12 50	1 42	2 55	2 59	5‡0	5 42	5 50	6 41	6 53	6 55	7 50	8 1	8 11	1014	..	1 54	8 29
19½	Dunstable Town	..	8 41	9 22	1 0	1 0	1 52	3 5	3 9	5‡9	5 51	5 59	6 50	7 3	7 5	8 0	8 11	8 21	1024	..	2 4	8 39
20½	" (L.M.R.) ... arr	..	8 44	9 27	1 5	1 5	1 57	3 10	3 14	5‡14	5 56	6 4	6 55	7 8	7 10	8 5	8 16	8 26	..	..	..	..
27½	¶ Leighton Buzzard arr	..	9 1	..	1 31	1 31	..	..	..	..	6 22	6 27	..	..	..	8 27	8 36	8 46	..	..	..	..

Miles		Week Days																	Sundays			
		a.m	a.m T	a.m	a.m	a.m	a.m	p.m S	p.m S	p.m E	p.m S	p.m	p.m E	p.m S	p.m S	p.m E	p.m J	p.m F	a.m		p.m	p.m
	¶ Leighton Buzzard dep	..	..	..	7 30	..	..	1254	1254	1254	..	..	..	..	5 38	5 38	7 45	7 45	..	..	..	..
—	Dunstable (L.M.R.) .. dep	5 55	..	6 58	7 53	..	9 38	1 15	1 27	1 50	2 35	3 25	5 23	5 23	6 25	6 25	8 32	8 37	..	..	..	..
1	" Town	6 0	..	7 3	7 57	..	9 43	1 20	1 31	1 54	2 40	3 30	5 28	5 28	6 30	6 30	8 37	8 42	8 0	..	2 30	6 16
5½	Luton arr	6 10	..	7 12	8 6	..	9 52	1 29	1 40	2 3	2 49	3 39	5 37	5 37	6 39	6 39	8 46	8 51	8 10	..	2 40	6 26
	Luton dep	..	6 42	7 16	..	8 14	9 57	1 30	..	..	2 54	3 42	6 0	6 0	6 55	7 0	8 51	8 56	8 15	..	2 45	6 31
8½	Luton Hoo H	..	6 48	7 22	..	8 20	10 3	1 35	..	..	3 0	3 49	6 6	6 6	7 1	7 6	8 57	9 2	8 22	..	2 51	6 38
10¾	Harpenden	..	6 54	7 28	..	8 26	10 9	1 41	..	..	3T8	3 57	6 12	6 12	7 7	7 12	9 3	9 8	8 27	..	2 57	6 44
13	Wheathampstead	..	7 0	7 33	..	8 32	1014	1 46	..	..	3 13	4 2	6 17	6 17	7 12	7 17	9 8	9 13	8 33	..	3 3	6 50
17¾	Welwyn Garden City	..	7 13	7 46	..	8§51	1027	1 59	..	..	3 26	4 16	6 30	6 31	7 28	7*35	9 21	9 26	8 46	..	3 16	7 3
20¼	Hatfield ... arr	..	7 21	7 55	..	8 57	1033	2 5	..	..	3 37	4 24	6F47	6 37	7 35	7*41	9 27	9 32	8 53	..	3 23	7 10
38	8a London (King's C.) arr	..	7 58	8L25	..	9N23	10B57	3L25	..	..	4P34	4BR47	7Z43	7B50	8 49	8A38	10 33	1033	9A50	..	4A15	8 18

A First and Third class between London (King's Cross) and Hatfield. B Change at Welwyn Garden City. First and Third class between London (King's Cross) and Welwyn Garden City. E Except Saturdays. F Fridays only. F Change at Welwyn Garden City. H Station for New Mill End. J Except Fridays. K Except Fridays and Saturdays. K Arr. 7 mins. *earlier*. L York Road (King's Cross). Change at Finsbury Park. N Arr. 9 40 a.m. on Saturdays. Change at Welwyn Garden City. First and Third class. P York Road (King's Cross). R 8 minutes later on Saturdays. S Saturdays only. T Through Train to King's Cross. T Arr. 3 mins. *earlier*. U Dep. 4 50 p.m. on Fridays. V Arr. 6 59 p.m. X Change at Finsbury Park also Welwyn Garden City. First and Third class between Finsbury Park and Welwyn Garden City. Z Change at Welwyn Garden City. Arr. York Road (King's Cross) 7 39 p.m. on Fridays. * 10 minutes later on Fridays. ‡ Runs 5 mins. *earlier* on Saturdays. § Arr. 6 mins. *earlier*. ‖ Arr. 5 5 p.m. (4 55 p.m. on Fridays).

June 1950

LEIGHTON BUZZARD

1.   This view from beside the former LNWR main line looks south towards the station. The left hand signals related to the Dunstable branch: the top signal protected the points on to the branch and the lower one was the fixed distant for signals controlled by Leighton No. 1 signalbox. (A. Vaughan coll.)

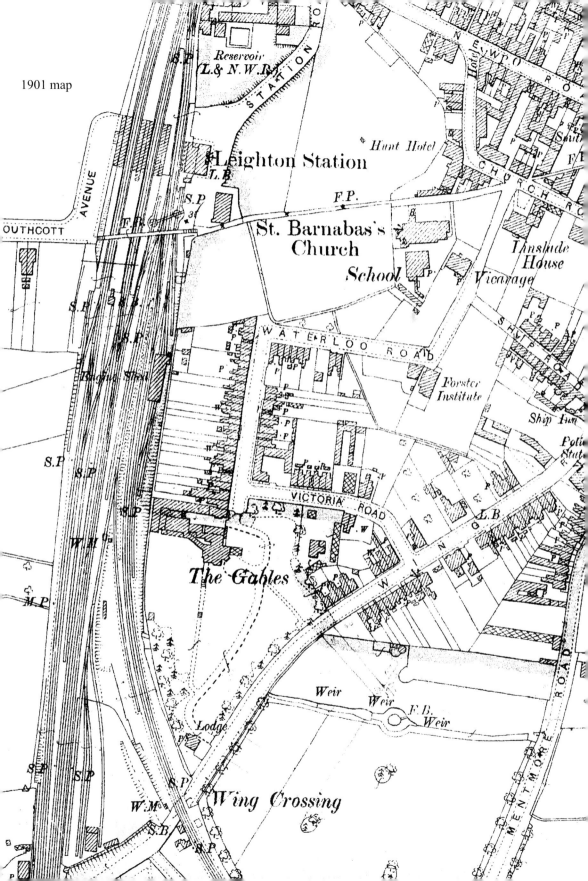

1901 map

2.   On 14th February 1859 this station opened to replace the original one built by the London & Birmingham Railway Company. It was sited "eight chains" south of the old station and at that time was only referred to as "Leighton", "Buzzard" being added from 1st July 1911. (A. Vaughan coll.)

3.   The station was just over forty miles from London (Euston) and in this general view, looking north, the Dunstable branch platforms are on the right. This and the next two photographs are from 1961. (A. Swain)

4.   Leighton No. 2 signalbox to the north of the station controlled entry on to the branch, but the actual branch signals were worked from Leighton No. 1 signalbox (on the main line south of the station). This glimpse into the interior of the latter in 1961 showed evidence of a well-maintained LNWR lever frame and polished linoleum. Note: the signalboxes were referred to simply as "Leighton", whereas station nameboards included "Buzzard". (A.Vaughan coll.)

5.   In this April 1961 broader view from the station, the main line disappears into the distance on the right, while a train of wagons stands in the adjacent Wing Yard sidings, laid in 1874 and closed in February 1967. The double track branch dropped down at 1 in 80, passed the engine shed which housed branch engines. The old coach to the left was used by staff and stood on a former private siding for Alders (Herbalists). (A.Swain)

6. A good head of steam announces the arrival of this short mixed freight train from Dunstable North, hauled by Stanier 8F 2-8-0 no. 48207. The engine shed, behind the train, closed in 1962 and here in August 1963 the roof had been removed and demolition was in progress. (G.I.Denn)

For other views of this station, please see *Watford to Leighton Buzzard.*

EAST OF LEIGHTON BUZZARD

7.　　In the shadow of the main line, Wing Road crossed the branch tracks, and here a signal box was built, capable of accommodating fifteen levers, but only five were installed, along with a gatewheel. The signal had been placed on the wrong side of the line to improve sighting round the sharp curve. (G.S.Woodward)

8.　　In October 1842 a small coal yard, known as Clay Cross Depot, opened in this area with a lime kiln, which, because it preceded the railway, was served by a tramway from the nearby Grand Junction Canal. This tramway was obliterated during the building of the branch but in 1853 the LNWR bought the coal depot and connected two sidings to it, worked from this signal box. On 31st December 1868 Daniel Carpenter, the gatekeeper, died after walking in front of a train. He had been working in excess of sixteen hours a day gatekeeping, shunting and coal unloading. A jury recommended staff hours should be cut - for the safety of passengers! (N.Mundy)

9.   A double-span girder bridge carried the branch over the Grand Junction Canal (later Grand Union) and the River Ouzel, at an appropriate level to allow for the passage of narrowboats beneath it. In order to achieve this, embankments were built leading up to the bridge, with gradients of 1 in 220 on either side. The canal company decreed that during the building of the railway there should be no interruption to boat movements. These waters have, on occasions, flooded this low-lying area. (G.S.Woodward)

10.   A relaxed moment was caught in this 1948 photograph, as the signalman pondered on the scene from his window and another member of staff rested on top of a wagon, while a train of sand wagons awaited its signal. In the centre, points allowed trains to run into the coal yard and in the distance the brickworks chimney stood proud. (A.Willmott)

11. To the left of this section of track, about a mile from Ledburn Crossing as it approached Grovebury, a siding ran off to connect with exchange sidings for the narrow gauge sandpit railway at Rackley Hill, but by 1969 this had disappeared. Between 1950 and 1957 British Railways built 1,000 steel 13-ton wagons to cater for the vast amount of traffic created by the extensive sand and gravel pits in this area. (G.S.Woodward)

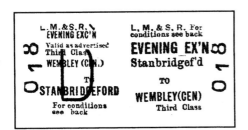

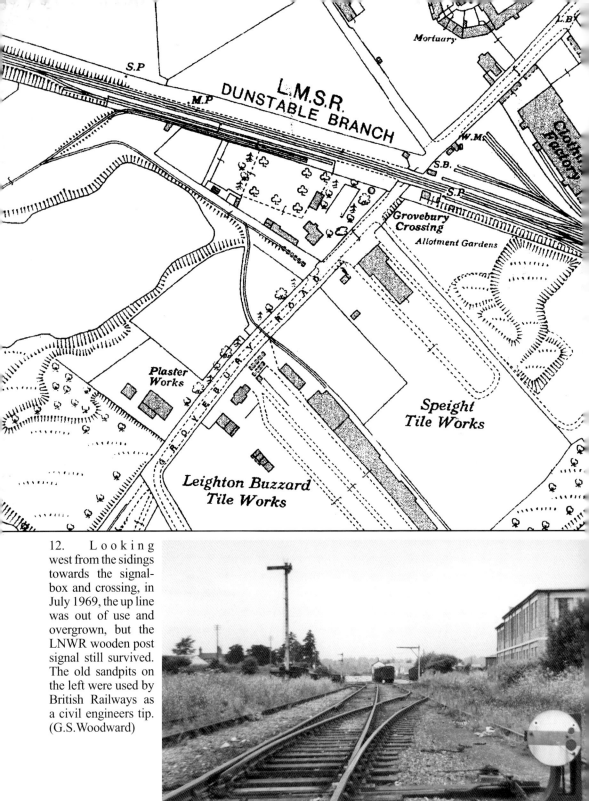

Labels on map:
S.P
M.P
L.M.S.R.
DUNSTABLE BRANCH
Mortuary
L.B.
W.M.
S.B.
Clothing Factory
S.P
Grovebury Crossing
Allotment Gardens
Plaster Works
GROVEBURY ROAD
Speight Tile Works
Leighton Buzzard Tile Works

12. Looking west from the sidings towards the signal-box and crossing, in July 1969, the up line was out of use and overgrown, but the LNWR wooden post signal still survived. The old sandpits on the left were used by British Railways as a civil engineers tip. (G.S.Woodward)

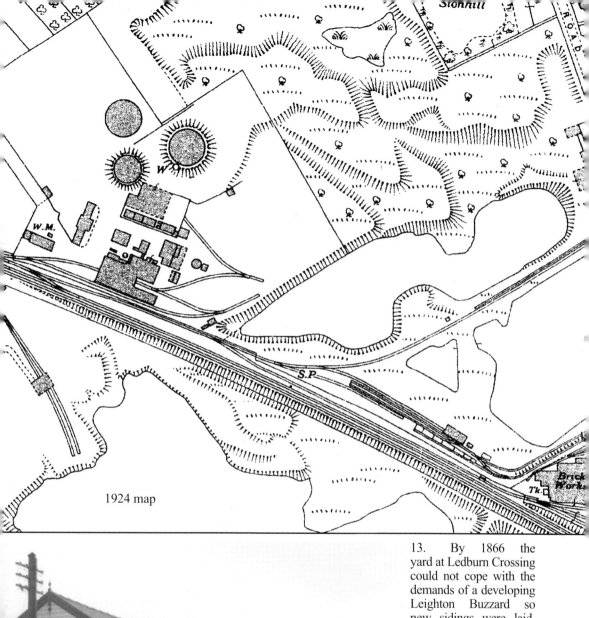

1924 map

13. By 1866 the yard at Ledburn Crossing could not cope with the demands of a developing Leighton Buzzard so new sidings were laid, at what was then known as Chapple's Crossing. The vans beyond the signalbox carried manufactured goods from Gossard's factory (behind the vans) and this siding also served the nearby gasworks. There was also a connection to exchange sidings with the sand pits narrow gauge railways on both sides of the branch. (G.S.Woodward)

14.　　Billington Road Crossing hut was built to shelter crossing keepers who manually operated the gates. It had fallen into ruin following closure of this section of the branch, but the six-lever frame outside was still in situ. The cupboard on the end of the building once housed signal repeaters. (G.S.Woodward)

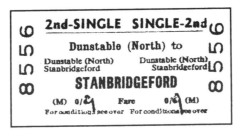

STANBRIDGEFORD

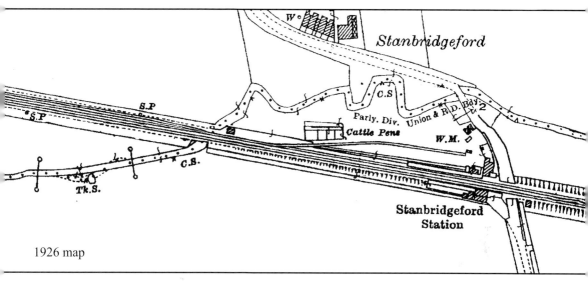

1926 map

15.   This LNWR eight-lever frame controlled the points and signals at the station. The lever in the reverse position, No. 4, was the level crossing gate lock and behind the frame was a diagram of signals and two repeaters for the distant signals. (G.I.Denn)

16.   Passengers were allowed to board and alight from trains at this point from about November 1849, but the station did not appear in public timetables until October 1860 when the platforms were constructed, incorporating old stone sleepers. By 1964 the station was beginning to take on an air of neglect, with the platform subsiding, but amazingly a seat bearing the station name had survived. (Authors coll.)

For other views of this station, please see
Watford to Leighton Buzzard.

17.   Looking east from the level crossing, the value of this little rural station for the conveyance of agricultural products, farm animals and market garden produce, such as strawberries and carnations, could well be appreciated. Gowers Siding was visible in the distance. The points in the foreground were controlled from the lever frame at the station. (G.S.Woodward)

18.   We are facing towards Dunstable in 1967, as the station awaited the demolition squad. Incredibly this compact collection of buildings and signals still exhibited something of their old character and charm, with wooden waiting rooms and decorative awnings. Gone were the days when the station was a popular destination for visitors seeking to explore the nearby Totternhoe Knolls. (G.I.Denn)

EAST OF STANBRIDGEFORD

19.   Just east of Stanbridgeford a siding served the Totternhoe
Lime & Stone Company quarries. Due to increased traffic, new
sidings and crossovers were installed in 1916, worked from a seven
lever ground frame beside a small cabin for the signalman and
the block instruments. In 1933 a signal box was erected over the
levers, at which time it became known as Gower & De Berenger
sidings (commonly shortened to Gower's). The connection to
sidings on the right led to an exchange siding. Here, in January
1969, the signalbox was being prepared for removal to Leighton
Buzzard Narrow Gauge Railway. (I.Bowley)

20.   At Totternhoe quarries, Sentinel locomotive no. 8 was making up a train of loaded chalk, the wagons having been lowered down a 1 in 10 rope-worked incline to the exchange sidings, where there was an engine shed. At times, up to five trains a day, with as many as 42 wagons per train, ran to Blisworth Sidings to be worked forward in shorter trains to Long Itchington, Warwickshire for cement manufacture. Increased costs brought an end to these movements on 15th April 1965. (G.I.Denn)

21.   Having almost reached the top of Sewell Bank LNWR 0-8-0 locomotive no. 49094 hauls its train of coal wagons towards Dunstable gasworks in April 1962. The 1 in 40 incline was almost 1¼ miles long. (G.I.Denn)

22.　　On 5th May 1962 Ivatt 2-6-2T no. 41289 propels a Leighton Buzzard to Dunstable North train through the deepest part of the cutting, dug into the escarpment of the Chiltern Hills, where, at the time the line opened, it was the steepest gradient on the whole of the LNWR system. The driver of this train was in the front of the leading coach, which was fitted with controls for pull and push working, while the fireman drove the locomotive. (G.I.Denn)

23.　　A sad sign of the times was caught on camera on 4th June 1962, when ex-LNWR 0-8-0 no. 49106 descended the bank with only a brake van, there being no wagons to return to Leighton Buzzard on this occasion. (G.I.Denn)

DUNSTABLE NORTH
LNWR Section

24.   Dunstable North station, known locally as "the lower station", became the meeting point of the two branches: the LNWR from Leighton Buzzard and the GNR branch from Hatfield, via Luton. A siding was laid in 1902 for the Dunstable Lime Company, which had a quarry near the top of the bank. This siding connected to the branch close to the level crossing at Brewer's Hill Road, where two more sidings were later added to serve Bedfordshire County Council's depot and Tar Oils Ltd. (Authors coll.)

25.   In September 1938, when war was considered almost inevitable, with air raids a possibility, the people of Dunstable were told to take consolation from the fact that a consignment of gas masks had been unloaded at the station. They were transferred to this LMS delivery lorry and taken to ARP headquarters for assembly. (Authors coll.)

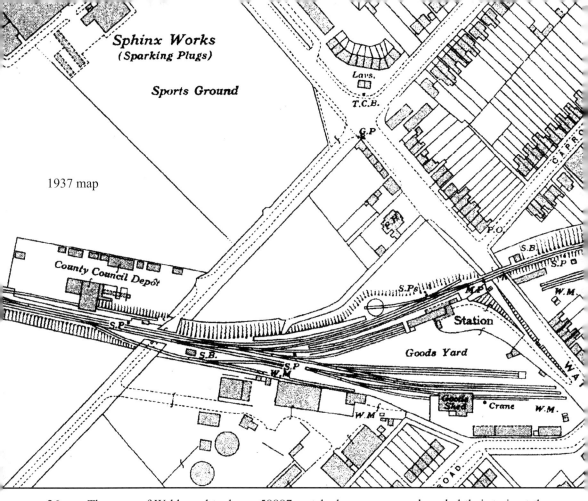

Sphinx Works
(Sparking Plugs)

Sports Ground

1937 map

County Council Depot

Lavs.
T.C.B.
G.P
S.B.
S.P
W.M.

Station

Goods Yard

Crane

W.M.

26.   The crew of Webb coal tank no. 58887 watched as passengers boarded their train at the bay platform. The lamp columns appeared to retain the remnants of their wartime paintwork, even though it was 1952. (G.Goslin)

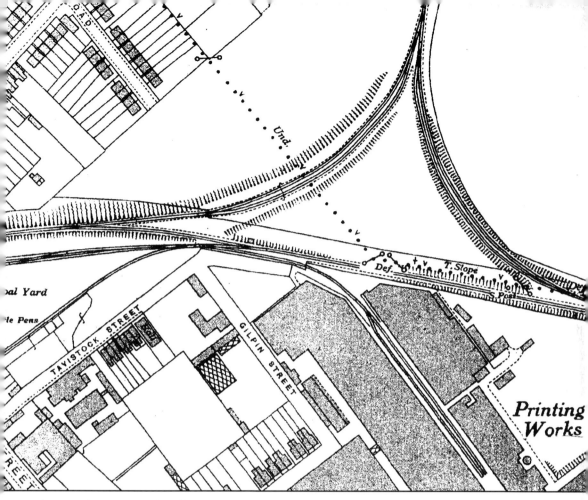

27.   The LNWR's signal box at Dunstable, pictured in 1957, stood on the south side of Brewer's Hill Road level crossing. To the rear of it, sidings served the gasworks and a coal storage area. (B.Parnall)

28.   While the main branch line curved round from the crossing to the station on the left, other tracks went straight on into the goods yard.This yard and a large goods shed had been built on the site of the original terminus station. The buildings to the right were part of the gasworks and in the left foreground, in 1957, workmen had commenced construction of a replacement signal box, as the old one on the opposite side of the tracks was suffering from subsidence. (B.Parnall)

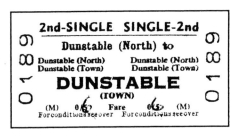

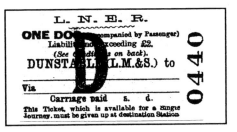

29.   The new Dunstable North signal box, with fifty levers, opened on 16th August 1958 and contained a gatewheel of Lancashire & Yorkshire Railway origin, which operated the crossing gates. A siding was laid into the gasworks in 1866, with a second added in 1937 which ran through separate gates in the foreground. The signal box closed on 23rd March 1969. (G.S.Woodward)

30.   About to descend Sewell Bank, this evening freight train of vans and tank wagons sets off for Leighton Buzzard, hauled by 8F 2-8-0 no. 48534 in June 1962. (G.I.Denn)

31.   This everyday scene concealed the fact that this was the last day of passenger service on the LNWR section, as Class 2, 2-6-2 tank engine no. 41222 waited with its pull and push train in the bay of the shared platform on 30th June 1962, although the official closing date was 2nd July. The fruit van on the left had been used as a parcel storeroom. (K.Taylor)

For other views of this station, please see *Watford to Leighton Buzzard.*

2nd-SINGLE   SINGLE-2nd

Stanbridgeford to

Stanbridgeford   Stanbridgeford
Luton (Bute Street)   Luton (Bute Street)

LUTON (Bute Street)

(M)   1/4   FARE   1/4   (M)

For conditions see over   For conditions see over

0571

DUNSTABLE NORTH
GNR Section

32.   From the viewing point of the bridge over Watling Street, an early photographer has managed to obtain a hazy image of Stirling J4 0-6-0 no. 387 as it waited with its train for Hatfield, beside the main platform in 1908. The original proposal was to cross this road on the level, but because of its importance as a coaching route, the railway company was forced to create an embankment and provide a bridge to enable their trains to run into the original LNWR station, and, from 1866, into this station. (Authors coll.)

33.   On the evening of 9th June 1951 the station presents a picture of activity with wagons in a siding and class 4F no. 44366 waiting to leave for Leighton Buzzard. To the left, Class N2 no. 69582 has arrived from Hatfield and, with the signal cleared, is about to run round its train. The station had "North" added to its title on 25th September 1950. (G.Goslin)

34. The driver of class N7, no. 69631 hands over the single line token at the end of his trip from Luton in May 1959. (A.Willmott)

↓ 35. The station was still lit by gas lamps in May 1963 when a two car DMU, destined for Hatfield, was being loaded with parcels. Locomotive D8025, with a brakevan, stands on the turntable siding. (G.I.Denn)

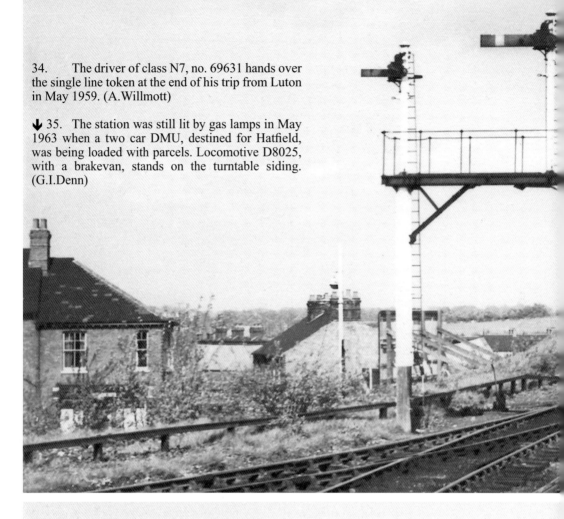

36.　　Associated Portland Cement Manufacturers Ltd had a large works at Houghton Regis. In October 1925 two sets of sidings were installed, forming a triangle with the branch, to bring in building materials for the new works, which opened the following year. The company initially ran its own fleet of steam engines around the works, but later employed diesels. Coal and gypsum arrived by the east side sidings and cement wagons left by the west side of the triangle. (G.S.Woodward)

37.　　Brush Traction Type 2 no. D5345 headed out of Dunstable in August 1963 and as it approached Dog Kennel Lane bridge it passed the eastern side of the cement works triangle. (G.I.Denn)

38.   The penultimate day of passenger services on this section was 23rd April 1965. An evening train for Hatfield awaits departure, carrying a South Beds Locomotive Club "Skimpot Flyer" headboard. This title had been adopted for one of its many organised railway excursions and was obviously seen as a fitting tribute from the society as services came to an end. (G.I.Denn)

39.   On the same day, this Cravens DMU, en route to Hatfield, was seen passing the site of the former GNR coal yard beside High Street North. The down home signal and the up starter were combined on a single post. (G.I.Denn)

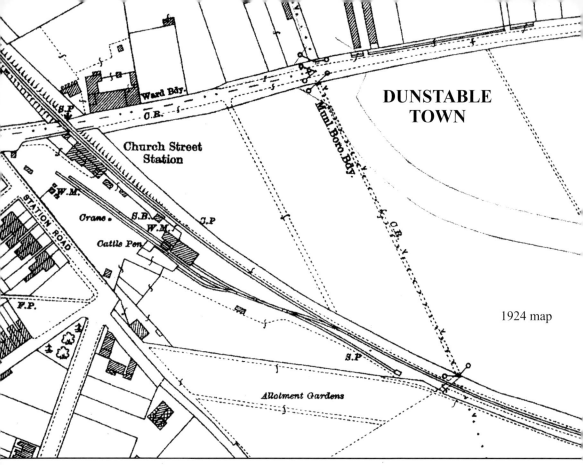

DUNSTABLE TOWN

Church Street
Station

1924 map

40.   With a train disappearing east into the countryside towards Skimpot, Blows Down was on the skyline. This postcard of about 1905 showed a notice on the signal box clearly titling this station as Dunstable Church Street, a name it retained until 1st January 1927, when it became Dunstable Town station. In November 1890 this signal box opened, after the platform had been lengthened, and it remained until 22nd July 1934, when a ground frame was installed to control the siding points. (Authors coll.)

41.   A mixed freight train from Hatfield was being shunted by N2 0-6-2T no. 69588 near the station in 1952. (H.Ramsey)

42.   The attractive wooden canopy over the platform was a feature of this station. The overall design was unusual in that whilst the main station facilities were at platform level, the entrance and booking office were on a lower floor with steps to connect the two. This view was taken from Luton Road bridge whilst it was being rebuilt in the 1960s. (G.Goslin)

43.   The station occupied a prominent position in the town, high above Luton Road, and from this angle the difference in levels between the entrance in the station yard and the platform could be appreciated. The recently rebuilt bridge spanned the busy main road (A505) and the buffers marked the end of the sidings when this photograph was taken on 18th January 1967. (H.Ramsey)

44.   In connection with Dunstable Carnival, a special shuttle service was run between Luton and Dunstable on 30th May 1968, when this well presented Cravens DMU was seen on its approach to the station. (H.Ramsey)

EAST OF DUNSTABLE

45.   A coal train is just about to pass over Skimpot Lane bridge, on its way to Dunstable Cement Works, and just visible behind the hedge on the left was a cold storage depot, built in 1941 for wartime supplies. (G.S.Woodward)

46.   This siding off the branch served the cold storage depot and on this very rare occasion a train was seen using it. (Authors coll.)

47.   Early in 1966 the London Railway Preservation Society began moving its rolling stock to the redundant storage depot siding. *Swanscombe*, an ex-Tunnel Cement locomotive built by Andrew Barclay in 1891, was photographed on 24th September 1967. Occasional steamings were held on site, prior to all the stock being moved to Quainton Road, near Aylesbury, in April 1969, which is now the Buckinghamshire Railway Centre. (A.Swain)

069   **G. N. R.**
Not transferable
DUNSTABLE L.& N. W. to
Dunstable L.& N.W.   Dunstable L.& N.W
DUNSTABLE CH. ST
DUNSTABLE Ch.St.   DUNSTABLE Ch.St.
Fare 2d.   First Class   Fare 2d.
Issued subject to the conditions stated on the back
hereof & on the Company's Time Bills & Notices.   069

176   **G. N. R.**
DUNSTABLE (L.&N.W.) to
DUNSTABLE(L.&N.W.)   DUNSTABLE (N.&N.W.)
DUNSTABLE (CHURCH STREET)
DUNSTABLE CH. ST.   DUNSTABLE CH. ST.
Fare 2d.   First Class   Fare 2d.
SEE CONDITIONS ON BACK.   176

CHAUL END

48.　　Although of poor quality (having been taken from a 1918 newspaper), inclusion was justified by it being the only known photograph of Chaul End station. It opened in 1915 and from 28th February 1916 LNWR trains stopped there, most of their passengers being female workers at the nearby Brown & Green's factory where they produced munitions. Shell filling was one of their main occupations and the women could easily be recognised at the end of their shift, by their dust covered orange faces. The five wagon length factory siding was taken out of use on 20th April 1916 and the station itself was demolished soon after closing in 1919. (Authors coll.)

49.　　On a beautiful day in September 1956, class N7 no. 69639 approaches the level crossing, where the token hoop was positioned in the exchange apparatus. The signal box closed on 1st November 1969. (S.Summerson)

EAST OF CHAUL END

50.   Central to this picture were points leading into a loop siding, laid in 1898, which later gave a connection to the private sidings of Laporte's chemical works. The company initially moved here to manufacture hydrogen peroxide for hat bleaching, but eventually dealt in other chemicals, bringing much varied traffic to their sidings. The ground frame that controlled the west end of the loop was removed early in 1972. The bridge carried waste from the works to a settling lagoon nearby. (G.S.Woodward)

51.   The chemical works employed two fireless locomotives for internal shunting, taking steam from their own supply. Here Andrew Barclay no. 2242/48 occupies the rails outside the engine shed on 14th July 1962. (A.Swain)

WEST OF LUTON

52.   This driver's view from a DMU, as the single track from Dunstable became double track through Luton, was taken in September 1962. The gantry on the right was used by Brown's timber yard to unload wagons on the steeply graded siding, while the siding on the left ran back to Maple Road coal yard. (G.S.Woodward)

53.　　　Several wagons were derailed during shunting near Luton Yard signal box at the entrance to the gasworks siding and a steam crane was needed to lift them back on the track. (K.Taylor)

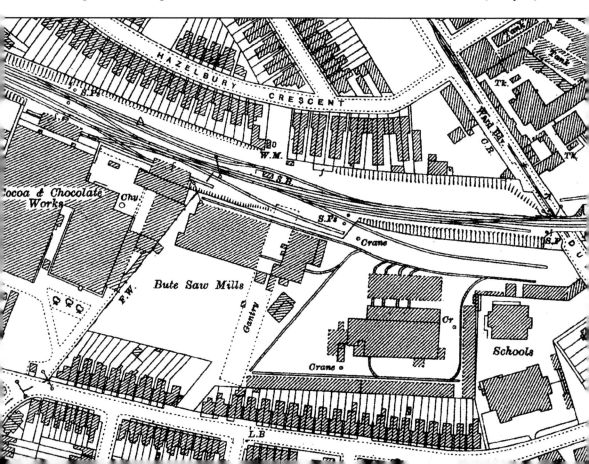

54.　　In 1964 this rare view of Luton Yard signal box (midway between Luton East and Luton West signal boxes) was taken from Station Road. It closed on 25th June 1967. The massive bulk of the goods shed towered above the line which, as part of a redevelopment of the station area in 1906, underwent a huge extension over the site of the old coal yard. (R.Flanagan)

1924 map

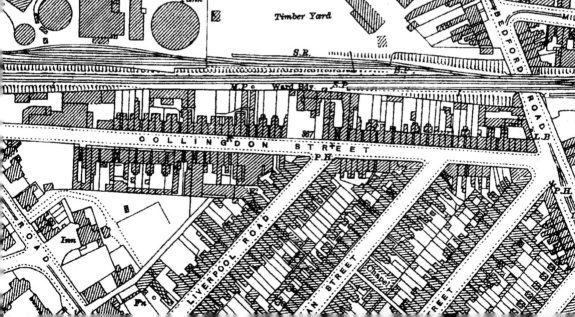

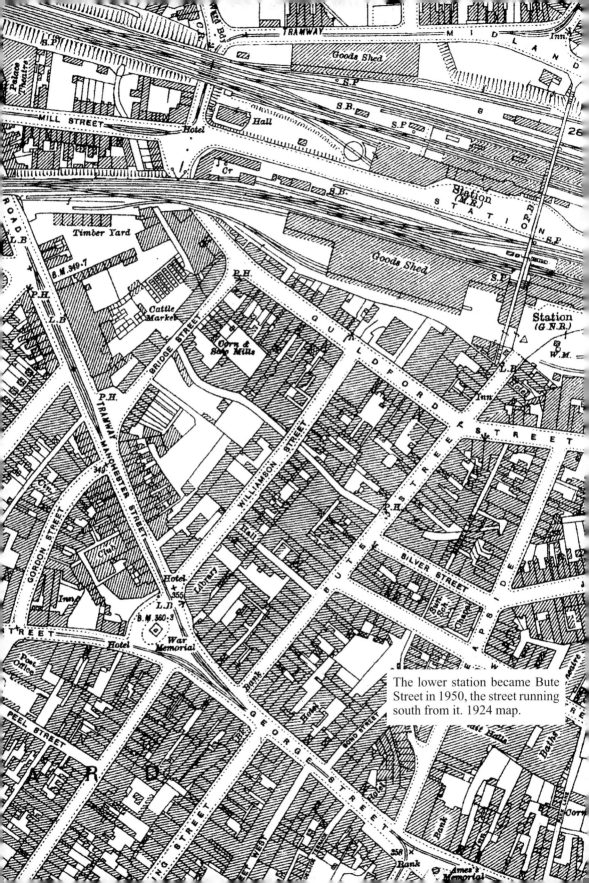

The lower station became Bute Street in 1950, the street running south from it. 1924 map.

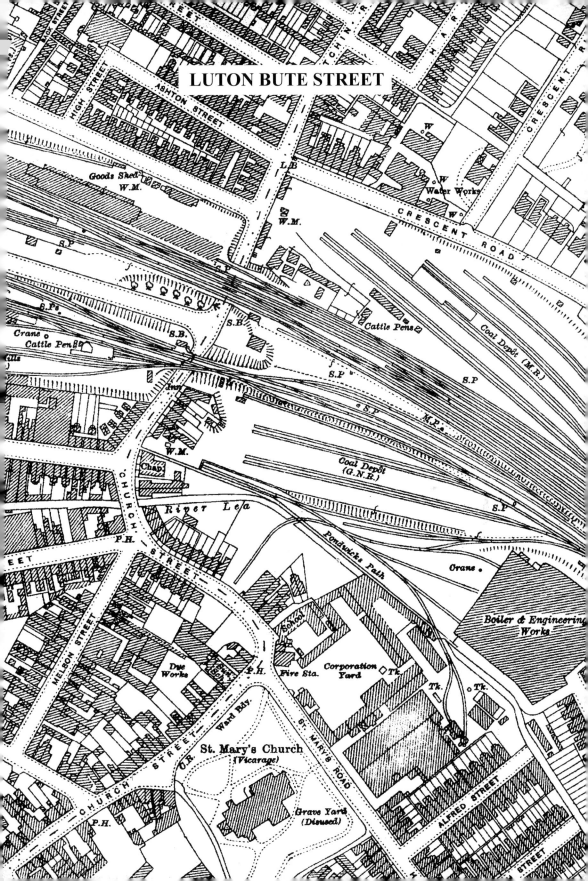

LUTON BUTE STREET

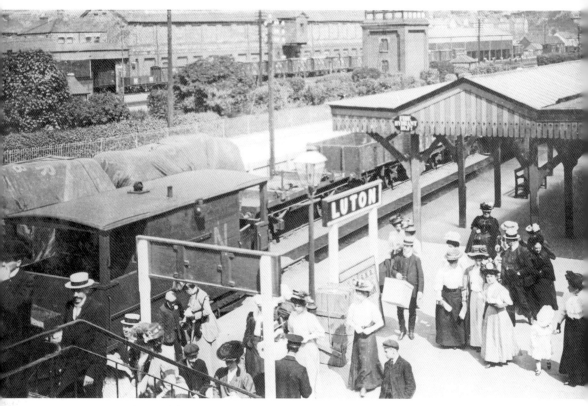

55.　　Across the road from the Midland station, passengers have arrived at the island platform of the GNR station, which opened on 3rd May 1858. On a summer day about 1906, the ladies' magnificent millinery and the gents straw boaters were evidence that this was a town famed for hat manufacture. The two tracks on the other side of this platform were basically used as a storage area for freight rolling stock. "Bute Street" was added to the station's title on 25th September 1950. (Authors coll.)

L.N.E.R.　(Series D)

6136

Not transferable. This ticket is issued subject to the notices & conditions in the Company's current time tables. AVAILABLE ON DAY OF ISSUE ONLY

LUTON to
DUNSTABLE(L.M.&S.)

Fare / S / 7½d.
THIRD 38 CLASS
DUNSTABLE L.M.&S.

6136

56.   Transferring vast amounts of hat boxes and crates between factories and the station kept the goods department's horses and carts very busy, as is evident in this pre-WWI photograph. In 1878 the Prince of Wales visited some of the factories and returned to London from this station. (Authors coll.)

L. N. E. R.   **PRIVILEGE**
(For conditions see back)
LUTON to
DUNSTABLE TOWN
Available within one week of date of issue
THIRD / S.P. \ CLASS
        38
DUNSTABLE TOWN
0300
0300

57.   A large forecourt gave access to the rather austere station building, with a notice on the front advertising the presence of a licensed station refreshment room, which was opened in 1886, but it became very dingy and a relic of a past era. However, it survived until the early 1960s. (K.Taylor)

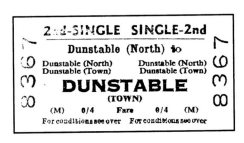

58.　　Near to the end of the so-called "Northern" platform was a water column, seen here in July 1956, with a "fire devil" brazier beneath it to keep the water frost free in winter. Class N2 0-6-2T no. 69639 had just taken on water. (G.Goslin)

59.　　An afternoon mixed freight train, hauled by class N2 0-6-2T no. 69594 running bunker first, simmered in the sunshine before leaving for Hatfield in 1959. (S.Summerson)

60.   Having arrived from Hatfield, class N7 0-6-2T no. 69698 is ready to reverse its train of coaches into the sidings to await their next tour of duty, under the watchful eye of the shunter in 1961. (S.Summerson)

61.   No. D5647 has brought its wagons to a halt beside the island platform on 19th August 1961. The guard is checking his train, which still included some wooden bodied wagons. By this time a section of roof awning had been removed from that platform. (A.Swain)

62.   All four lines were occupied in August 1963, a freight train being in the siding and a set of quad-art coaches stood alongside the "Northern" platform. Beside the main platforms two Cravens DMUs waited before setting off in opposite directions. (A.Swain)

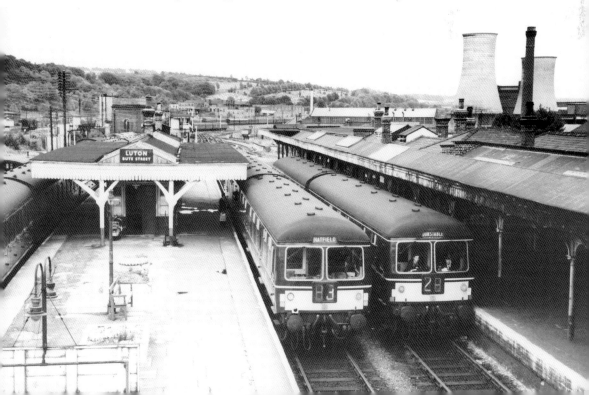

63.   Prior to heading up "The Cobbler" excursion, the engine took on water from the column at the north end of the platform. The driver controlled the valve and the fireman held the bag in the tank. The footbridge overhead linked the Midland main line station and the Dunstable branch station with Bute Street itself giving access to Luton town centre. (G.I.Denn)

For photographs of Luton Midland Road station, please see *St. Albans to Bedford*.

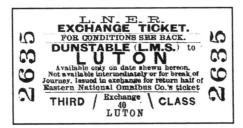

64.   A credit to the cleaners, the shining class 4F 0-6-0 no. 44414 is about to back on to "The Cobbler" special train, organised by the South Beds Locomotive Club, for its run to Northampton on 19th September 1964. (G.I.Denn)

65.   On 24th April 1965, the last day of service for passenger trains on the Great Northern section, a Dunstable bound train passed D8046 working a train for Hatfield, watched by a policeman and some enthusiasts. (G.I.Denn)

EAST OF LUTON

← 66. Looking in an easterly direction in 1947, the fireman of a Hatfield bound train receives the single line staff from the signalman at the old GNR signal box. The boarded area across the track provided a safe standing area during the changeover. (G.Goslin)

67. This coal train arrives from Hatfield in September 1959, hauled by class N7, 0-6-2T no. 69678 from Hatfield shed. The newly built signal box stood ready to take over the work of the adjacent signal box after it suffered from subsidence. (S.Summerson)

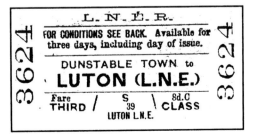

L.N.E.R. (Series C)
NOT TRANSFERABLE. This ticket is issued subject to the General Notices, Regulations and Conditions in the Company's current Time Tables, Book of Regulations and Bills. Available for three days, including day of issue
8248
DUNSTABLE TOWN to
LUTON
Fare / S 39 \ 6½d.
THIRD CLASS
LUTON
8248

L.N.E.R.
FOR CONDITIONS SEE BACK. Available for three days, including day of issue.
3624
DUNSTABLE TOWN to
LUTON (L.N.E.)
Fare / S 39 \ 8d.C
THIRD CLASS
LUTON L.N.E.
3624

68.　　By this time, the last remaining traffic on the branch was coal for Dunstable cement works, with return loads of tank wagons containing their finished products. On 10th July 1969 the locomotive has pushed its wagons backwards, ready to use a new connection to the Midland main line, opened in January 1966, when the route to Hatfield closed. The signal box closed on 15th December 1969 and the remainder of the branch was then worked as a siding from Luton South signal box on the Midland main line. (G.S.Woodward)

69.　　Approaching Luton from the east, sidings fanned out from the headshunt to serve the coal yard which had been built as part of the GNR 1906 redevelopment. Also, a private siding ran into the electricity power station, which owned a four-wheeled battery electric locomotive, built by Greenwood & Batley in 1931, to shunt their siding. (R.Flanagan)

70.	This train for Hatfield has passed Vauxhall Motors' works and was viewed from Park Corner on Lower Harpenden Road, east of Luton in about 1960. Having moved to Luton in 1905 as a small company, Vauxhall Motors Ltd was formed in 1907. Their factory was served by sidings, which extended east as far as the bridge under the first coach. (Authors coll.)

71.	Vauxhall's sidings were laid in 1941, joining a siding serving a nearby electricity substation. Coal came in for the power house and in WWII military vehicles and tanks built in the factory were taken away by rail. Later on, crated vehicles and parts were despatched by rail for export, as illustrated here in 1962. A D8000 class locomotive passes by with its passenger train from Dunstable. (K.Taylor)

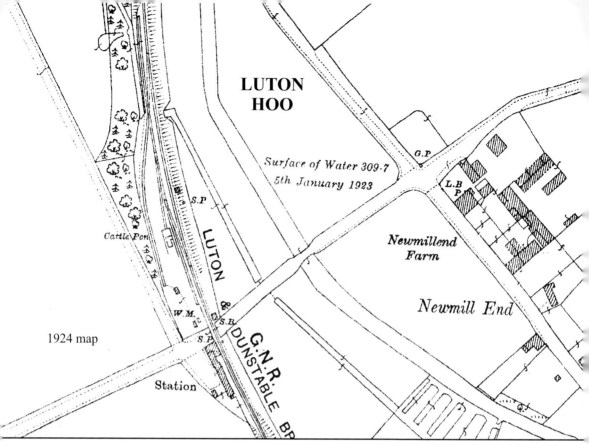

LUTON HOO

Surface of Water 309.7
5th January 1923

Cattle Pen

S.P

LUTON

W.M.

S.B

S.P

G.N.R.

DUNSTABLE BR

Station

1924 map

G.P.

L.B P

Newmillend Farm

Newmill End

72.   The line skirted round the perimeter of Luton Hoo Park and was mostly hidden by trees. To conceal the branch from Luton Hoo residents the GNR had built a short length of screen wall, but when the Midland main line was built some years later, at a much higher level immediately above the branch, a vast retaining wall was needed to support it and no attempts were made to hide that line from view. (G.Goslin)

73.   The station opened on 1st September 1860 under the name of New Mill End. John Leigh of Luton Hoo arranged with the GNR that trains would stop here at his request, but in 1861 the company refused to renew the agreement. The station was renamed Luton Hoo on 1st December 1891. Here it is viewed from the Lower Harpenden Road about 1925. At this time a signal box was still in use beside the level crossing. (Authors coll.)

74.   This photograph was taken after the signal box had been removed in 1930, but before a sewerage works was built in the field north of the station in 1941. The station dealt with most of Luton Hoo estate's goods traffic, with the rest being handled by Chiltern Green station on the Midland main line in the distance. The building to the left of the crossing was a weighbridge hut. (Authors coll.)

75.   This general view of the sidings west of the level crossing shows the cattle dock and coal storage area. The sidings closed in November 1963. (Authors coll.)

76.   A passenger train from Dunstable passes over the level crossing and into the station in 1962. The station canopy sheltered the platform and extended back to cover an area of the station forecourt, to provide cover for carriages from Luton Hoo house, as they delivered or collected their notable visitors. (Authors coll.)

SOUTH OF LUTON HOO

77.   The Midland main line was quadrupled in the 1890s, necessitating the building of a second bridge to carry the new tracks over the Dunstable branch. This photograph dates back to about 1894, with everything new and neat. (Authors coll.)

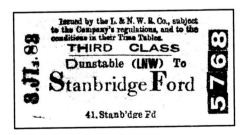

78.   This preserved locomotive, GNR no. 1247, hauled several excursion trains over the line and here on 14th April 1962 it passes East Hyde with a special train for Luton, run by the Stephenson Locomotive Society. (Authors coll.)

79.   Moving east, Hyde Mill had a siding which was installed in 1865 to serve this large storage shed where seed potatoes and other farm produce were kept. The sleeper built buffer marking the end of the siding was still standing beside the rather derelict shed in 1968, but the track had been removed in 1962. (L.Casey)

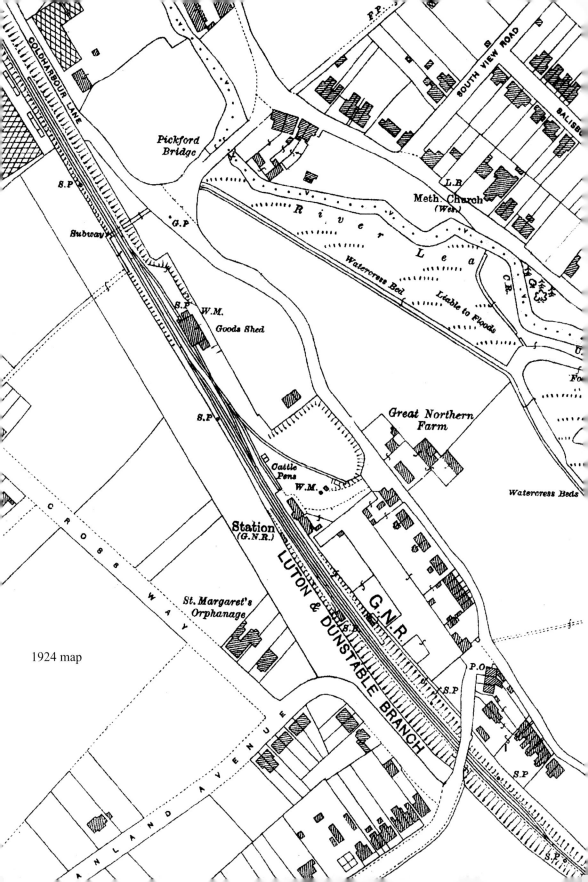

1924 map

HARPENDEN EAST

80.   Looking west in the direction of Luton, in about 1936, the station presented a neat appearance, with a boldly painted nameboard. The van in the centre was standing beside the cattle dock and beyond that a siding ran into the goods shed. The station's oil lamps were replaced by electric lights in 1937. The station had a name change on 25th September 1950, when it became Harpenden East. (N.Bridger)

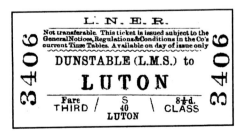

81.   LNER locomotive no. 3011 shunts in the goods yard in July 1936, with a coal wagon, owned by Goddard & Rudd of Luton, being placed in the back coal road. (J.M.Jarvis)

82.   The branch was often used by special trains for supporters attending Luton Town Football Club matches. Here, as it passed the cattle dock siding in September 1958, one of those trains was on its way back to London. (G.S.Woodward)

83.   When the signal box was switched out, up trains passed over the down line through the station, as seen here on 14th March 1959. The goods yard processed a great variety of products including coal and coke from Luton gasworks, manure from London Zoo and fuel for the nearby Randall's nursery (which dispatched large quantities of tomatoes, cucumbers and lettuce in season) and watercress from the local beds. Cattle, horses, fertilisers and other agricultural produce came and went through this small station. (G.S.Woodward)

84.   One of the first diesel locomotives to run on the line is seen at the station in June 1959, with a Dunstable train, direct from London. However, most trains were still hauled by steam locomotives at this time. (G.S.Woodward)

85.   The spacious signal box contained thirty levers and was built by McKenzie & Holland of Worcester. Heating and cooking facilities came from a coal fired range and along the back was a desk and a working area where signal lamps could be cleaned and trimmed. (Authors coll.)

86.　　In January 1963 the country experienced severe winter conditions, with hard frost and heavy snow, which blocked the branch near Ayot and left this up goods train stranded in the passing loop at Harpenden. A snow plough made up of an old steam engine tender pushed by a diesel locomotive, forced its way through and is seen here returning to Hatfield. (G.S.Woodward)

87.　　Looking from Station Road bridge, towards the east end of the passing loop, one could obtain a good view of the up starting signal, with co-acting arms on a concrete post, whereas the down line signal beyond had a lattice post. (R.Flanagan)

EAST OF HARPENDEN

88.   Leaving the town behind, the line ran beside the parkland of the Aldwickbury estate. Harpenden distant signal dominated the landscape and a brick platelayers hut was almost hidden by bankside foliage. (G.S.Woodward)

L. N. E. R.
For conditions see back
Available for three days including day of issue.

Luton Hoo
LUTON HOO
WHEATHAMPSTEAD
W'HAMPSTEAD

3rd. 1s. 0d.Z

L. N. E. R.
For conditions see back
Available for three days including day of issue.

Luton Hoo to
Luton Hoo
WHEATHAMPSTEAD
W'HAMPSTEAD

3rd. 1s. 0d.Z

0433   0433

89.   Following withdrawal of a Sunday passenger service as from 21st January 1951, a designated newspaper train had to be run to Luton each Sunday morning and here the locomotive that hauled one of those trains gently approaches *Leasey Bridge* crossing on its return journey in 1957. (G.S.Woodward)

90.   In latter days, the level crossing gates were normally against rail traffic, so crossing keepers relied on being told of approaching trains by telephone, usually getting the gates open in time. However, in one week the gates were damaged on two occasions! (Authors coll.)

91.   This double span low girder bridge took the branch line over the River Lea as it flowed through a particularly marshy area with reed beds, just west of Wheathampstead. (G.S.Woodward)

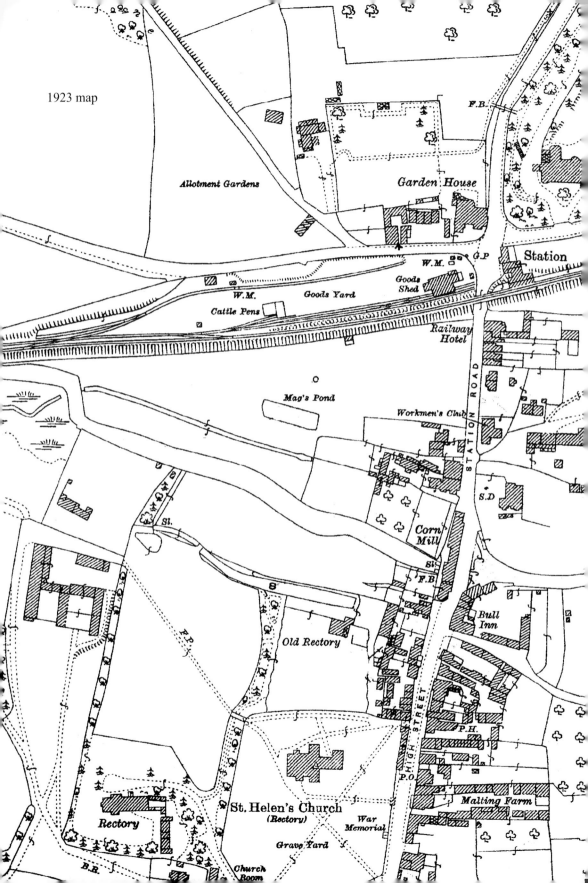

1923 map

Allotment Gardens

Garden House

F.B.

Station

G.P.

W.M.

W.M.

Goods Yard

Goods Shed

Cattle Pens

Railway Hotel

Mag's Pond

Workmen's Club

STATION ROAD

S.D.

Corn Mill

St.

F.B.

St.

F.P.

Old Rectory

Bull Inn

HIGH STREET

P.H.

Rectory

P.O.

St. Helen's Church
(Rectory)

War Memorial

Malting Farm

Grave Yard

B.R.

Church Room

WHEATHAMPSTEAD

92.   It was necessary to build a high embankment in order to put a bridge over Station Road and consequently the station was perched on top of this earthwork, which is not evident from this old postcard, although the train from Luton does appear to be climbing as it passes over the bridge and approaches the platform. (Authors coll.)

93.   Although the details of this (presumably) military event are not known, a fine body of men and musicians has gathered outside the station master's house at the end of Station Road. The small building attached to the house was, until 1881, the original booking office and passengers gained access to the station, high up on the right, by a flight of steps. The station's cattle pen was removed in the run up to closure of the line, so when a cow arrived soon after, it was delivered to the platform and led down the steps, but it suddenly took fright and careered off with a porter clinging to its tail. The animal was eventually rounded up and delivered to a local farm. (Authors coll.)

94. Looking east in about 1960, the station platform extends as far as a bridge over the intriguingly named Waddling Lane. The playwright, George Bernard Shaw, was a local resident but a bad timekeeper, so his chauffeur often had to rush up the steps to halt the train's departure until Shaw arrived. The pipeline on the right ran directly from Murphy Chemicals' factory to the goods yard. This company came to Wheathampstead in 1932 and, as a result, part of the loading dock was covered to keep their products dry. (G.Goslin)

L. N. E. R.
FOR CONDITIONS SEE BACK. Available for three days, including day of issue.
WHEATHAMPSTEAD to
CAMBRIDGE
Fare / S \ 6s.6d.C
THIRD 35 CLASS
CAMBRIDGE
0230 0230

95.   As a Dunstable train descended the embankment from the station in September 1962, it passed the goods shed. The goods yard, complete with a cattle dock and a stable, was situated at a low level, on the west side of Station Road, where there were two sets of points into the sidings, allowing shunting from both directions. These were controlled from a signal box until September 1921, when ground frames were installed. (G.S.Woodward)

96.   After the line was closed to passengers, a replacement bus service (Route No. 366) was provided betwen Luton and Welwyn Garden City, seen here as it passed under Station Road railway bridge, which was later removed. (Authors coll.)

EAST OF WHEATHAMPSTEAD

97.   Blackbridge landfill dump was formerly a gravel pit, first excavated in 1887. As the gravel was removed, London refuse was brought into these sidings and distributed around the site via a two foot gauge railway, in latter days using three Simplex locomotives. George Bernard Shaw often complained to the local Council about the stench that drifted over his house from this site, saying he was reminded not of Shakespeare's "thyme and violet scented bank" but of "Stromboli and Hell"! The siding closed on 24th May 1971. (Authors coll.)

98.   Out in the countryside east of the gravel workings, class N2 0-6-2T no. 69648 steamed through with its Dunstable bound passenger train on 30th August 1958, having just passed under Sparrowhall Bridge, near Waterend. (Authors coll.)

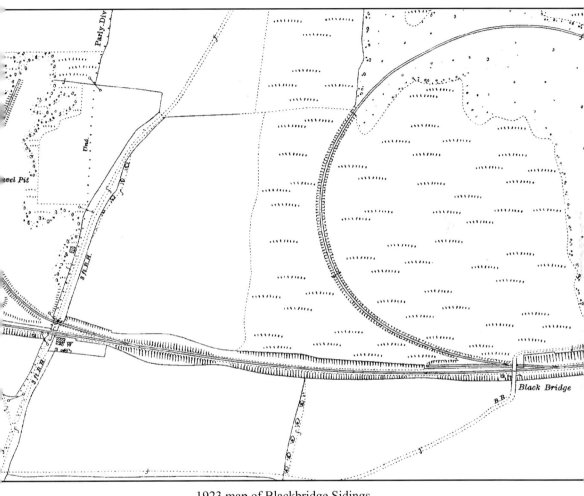

1923 map of Blackbridge Sidings.

AYOT

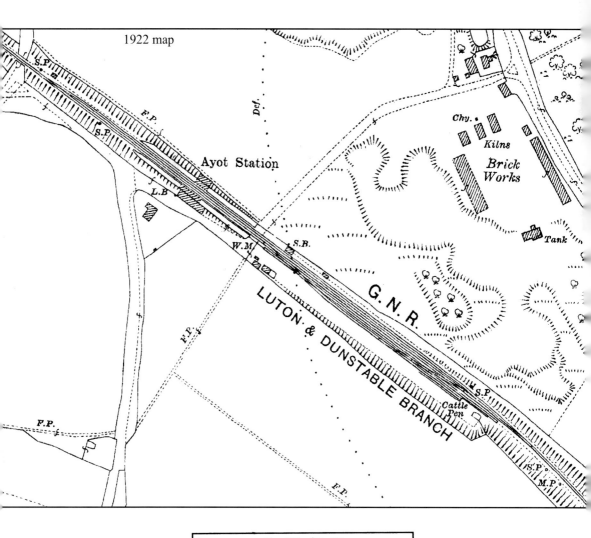

1922 map

S.P.
F.P.
S.P.
Ayot Station
L.B
W.M.
S.B.
Def.
Chy.
Kilns
Brick Works
Tank
G.N.R.
LUTON & DUNSTABLE BRANCH
Cattle Pen
S.P.
S.P.
M.P.
F.P.
F.P.
F.P.

99.	Looking west from the signalbox, this little timber-built station (initially titled Ayott St. Peter, until its name change on 1st April 1878) presented a neat and clean appearance. The large building on the left, at the bottom of the approach road, was the station masters house. (D.White)

100.	Down at platform level, facing east in about 1920, it was possible to appreciate just how far the canopies extended out, with their decorative woodwork having been shaped to clear the trains. The signal box opened in 1892, when the passing loop was installed. Among the goods handled by this station were coal, corn and soft red bricks made locally in Deard's brickfield. In snowy weather, passengers would change their shoes at the station and leave their gum-boots in the waiting room, for their return home. (Authors coll.)

101.   On 26th July 1948, most of the buildings were destroyed by fire, thought to have been started by a spark from a passing train. This sad image of the booking office clearly indicated the extent of the devastation. (D.White)

102.   A freight train, on its way to Hatfield, in August 1955, has passed the two sidings and the coal yard, from which local coal merchants traded. (G.Goslin)

103.   About to leave the passing loop, this train was heading east towards Welwyn Garden City, under the Great North Road (A1). The down home signal had to be tall so that it could be seen above the bridge. (G.Goslin)

EAST OF AYOT

104.   An empty refuse train, made up of sulphate and mineral wagons, returns from Blackbridge sidings on 13th December 1967, past the site of the goods yard. (R.Hummerston)

105.   Class N7 0-6-2T no. 69617 struggles its way up Ayot Bank through Brocks Wood with a passenger train for Dunstable, on 4th July 1953, having left behind the down distant signal. This was a 1 in 56 gradient, where a banking engine was sometimes needed and wagon numbers were restricted. Primroses flowered in the wood in the Spring. (G.Goslin)

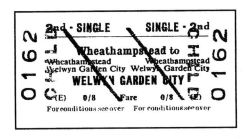

106.   A type 1 diesel locomotive rounds the curve into the cutting past Digswell Junction cottages and under Digswell Road bridge (known as the White Bridge), which was No. 1 on the branch. The banner repeater indicated the position of a signal out of sight further round the curve. (Authors coll.)

107.   This Type 2 locomotive, no. D5614, hauls its train of covered wagons, containing Islington's refuse, via Ashburton Grove and Ayot Bank (near Handside Lane) to Blackbridge sidings on a snowy day just after Christmas in 1968. (R.Hummerston)

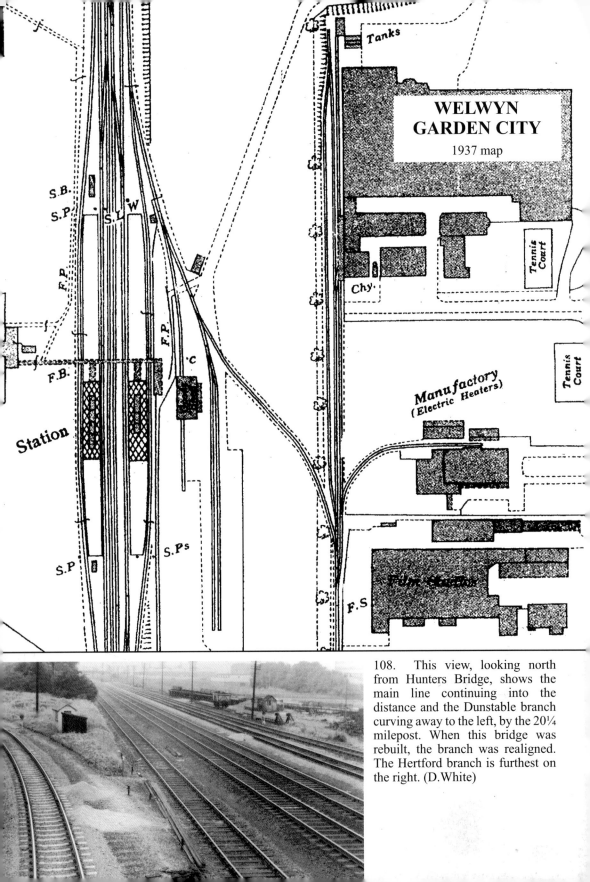

WELWYN GARDEN CITY

1937 map

Tanks

Tennis Court

Chy.

Tennis Court

Manufactory
(Electric Heaters)

S.B.

S.P.

S.L.W

F.P.

F.P.

C

F.B.

Station

S.P.

S.Ps

F.S

108. This view, looking north from Hunters Bridge, shows the main line continuing into the distance and the Dunstable branch curving away to the left, by the 20¼ milepost. When this bridge was rebuilt, the branch was realigned. The Hertford branch is furthest on the right. (D.White)

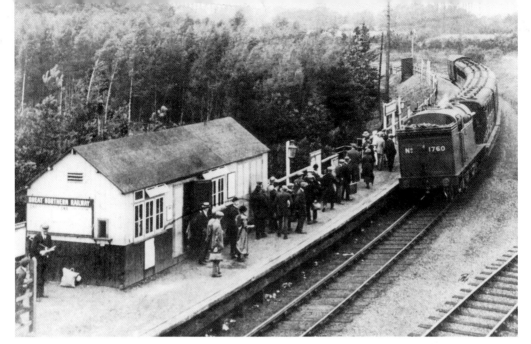

109. With the coming of Ebenezer Howard's Garden City (later renamed as Welwyn Garden City), a temporary passenger platform was constructed on the curve near where the branch ran out from the Kings Cross main line and this came into use on 16th August 1920. A chartered train conveyed the new town's construction workers from and to London each day and most of the building materials were handled through Horn's Siding nearby. (D.White)

110. To replace the temporary wooden halt, a new station (200 yards to the south) was brought into use on 20th September 1926, although it was officially opened by Mr. Neville Chamberlain on 5th October. This N2 0-6-2T class no. 69534, is ready to depart for Dunstable with the 6.07 train from Hatfield, in June 1951. The footbridge in the background not only connected the station platforms, but also served as a public footpath over the railway, on payment of a toll. (Authors coll.)

111.   A cross platform connection was made between main line trains and branch services. This double-headed branch line train is seen in May 1959. (A.Wilmott)

For other views of Welwyn Garden City and Hatfield please see *Potters Bar to Cambridge*

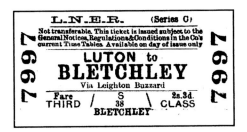

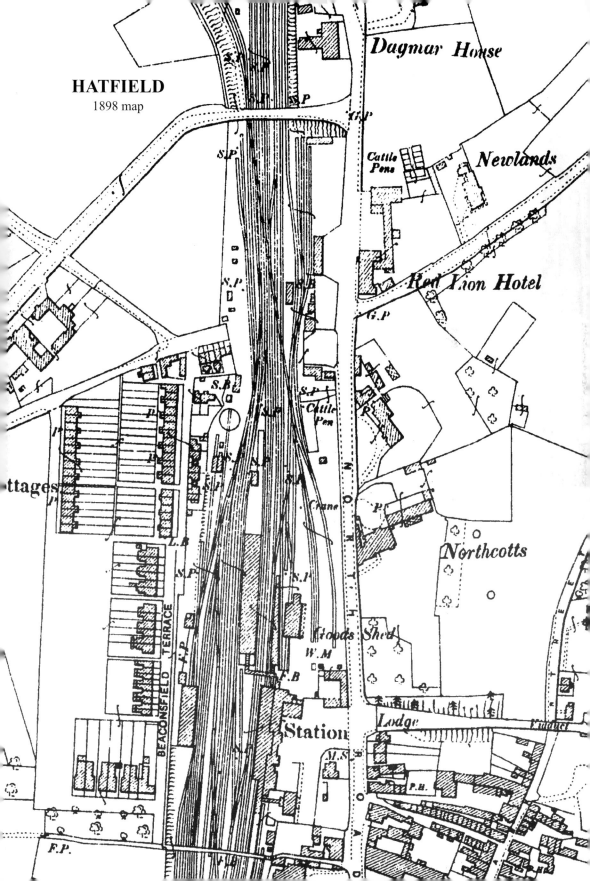

HATFIELD
1898 map

Dagmar House

Newlands

Cattle Pens

Red Lion Hotel

Northcotts

Goods Shed

Station

Lodge

BEACONSFIELD TERRACE

ttages

Crane

Cattle Pen

112. Looking south from Stanborough Lane bridge, 20th Mile Down Signal Box cast a lonely shadow in the exceptionally well maintained cutting. It was built in 1895 and had twenty-five levers to control trains in the down direction, but closed in 1926 when the new signal box opened at Welwyn Garden City. Dunstable trains used the track on the right. (K.Ladbury)

113. LNER 4-4-0 locomotive no. 4323 was used for branch trains, and is positioned on the turntable in August 1924. In the background are some railway staff houses. (K.Ladbury)

114. An error of judgement resulted in this locomotive over-running and falling into the empty turntable pit, after the table had been taken out to be repaired in 1955. (D.Moretti)

115.   On 20th February 1966 engineering work caused the subsidence of part of Wrestlers Bridge (which carried the A1 Great North Road over the railway) and it had to be demolished. The Dunstable branch was blocked, so a connection was put in between the down goods line and the branch at Welwyn Garden City to enable refuse trains to reach Blackbridge sidings. It came into use on 15th May 1966 and the remainder of the line to Hatfield was eventually lifted. In the meantime refuse trains ran to Holwell tip on the former Hertford branch. (Authors coll.)

116.   As a brakedown train made its way north on the main line, behind it stood a number of wagons containing crated vehicles from Vauxhall Motors at Luton. Dominating the skyline are the Dunstable branch signals: those on the left allowed access on to the main line, the centre signals allowed trains to access Hatfield's western platform and the right hand signals controlled access into the sidings. (Authors coll.)

117.   From the north end of the station, Hatfield No. 3 signal box (built about 1896 with 80 levers) had set up the points on the right hand track for trains to Luton and Dunstable to cross over to the branch track. No. 2 box is opposite and was involved with Dunstable-London trains. (T.Murphy)

118.   A Cravens DMU waits beside the Dunstable line platform, known as the Western platform, with the engine shed and some tank wagons for Laporte's chemical works on the right of the picture. (R.Flanagan)

119.   This Dunstable bound DMU made its way off the main line and into Hatfield station in January 1961, just after closure of the engine shed. Redundant steam locomotives were being stored on the tracks furthest away and the nearer sidings were filled with a variety of goods wagons. (Authors coll.)

120.   In 1941 a connection was put in to allow trains from London to use the down slow line, giving direct access to the branch platform and permitting through running of trains from London to Dunstable. This signal gantry on the main line, south of Hatfield station, was altered accordingly. Through trains in the opposite direction crossed over north of the station. Sadly all was lost, but this image serves as a reminder of a former way of railway life. (R.Brown)

Middleton Press

EVOLVING THE ULTIMATE RAIL ENCYCLOPEDIA

Easebourne Lane, Midhurst, West Sussex.
GU29 9AZ   Tel:01730 813169

www.middletonpress.co.uk   email:info@middletonpress.co.uk
A-978 0 906520 B- 978 1 873793 C- 978 1 901706 D-978 1 904474 E - 978 1 906008

OOP Out of print at time of printing - Please check availability   BROCHURE AVAILABLE SHOWING NEW TITLES